KEYS TO SUSTAINABLE Small & Medium Enterprises (SMEs)

By

Chiedu Okonta

Dedication

This work is dedicated to the Holy Spirit, who is the ultimate source of inspiration! It is further dedicated to my key mentors- Bishop David Oyedepo and Tony Elumelu **(C.O.N)** whose work and dedication have been our great source of inspiration.

I also dedicate this to my lovely wife- Rosemary and my children Ebube, Olivia, Ugo and Chidera for their sacrifices in allowing us go the extra mile for this book. Of course, also dedicated to my main industrialist mentor in Ghana- Nana Dr M.A. Addo.

Contents   Pages

1. Why Sustainable SMEs?..7
2. Basic foundation for an SME 11
3. The key product or services for the SME 13
4. Fundamental principles of accounting & HR 17
5. The SME Income and Expenditure account 21
6. The SME Balance Sheet 23
7. Effective Management of the Assets 25
8. Effective Management of the Liabilities 33
9. Making the best from banking loans 35
10. Optimal handling of SME taxation issues 37
11. Cash flow analysis 42
12. SME cash cycle 47
13. Best Investments Handling Procedure 58

PREFACE

Many businesses, especially SMEs with very great visions and expectations, unfortunately, are not able to successfully survive their initial 5 years of operations. Statistics has it that about 65% of business start-ups do not live beyond 5 years. While most of the businesses that survived beyond 5 years end up struggling as petty businesses until they eventually go into extinction. A lot of efforts and resources are involved in setting up every business, hence, should not be wasted, but nurtured to produce the best results!

As a Chartered Accountant and a Banker for over two decades, we had to provide financial services and guidance to some Small and Medium Establishments, and have seen a lot of them witness tremendous growth within a very short space of time. It was noticed in particular that the entities which implemented those pieces of guidance have become very successful with ease. This compilation is to put down **some of the key points** *that have been the success factors for their speedy and sustainable growth.*

This book makes it clear that every genuine business has the chances of not just being successful, but becoming a great business entity within a short period of time. It is thus highly recommended for every existing and aspiring Small & Medium Establishments **(SMEs)**. *It is equally necessary for under-graduates with business aspiration, who do not want to experience the unnecessary pitfalls previous SMEs encountered. It could also guide the Lecturers and Teachers handling business classes. Most importantly, this book is conceived to support the forward-looking* **Africapitalism aspiration** *of Tony Elumelu (C.O.N) Foundation, in his quest to raise millions of African Young Entrepreneurs!*

The book is carefully packaged in a very simplified form, such that irrespective of one's background, every user should have good understanding of basic financial management principles required to achieve sustainable SME growth.

FORWARD

Small and Medium Scale Enterprises (**SMEs**) are significant contributors to the development of countries all over the world; especially in developing countries. SMEs also employ greater number of people than any other sector in the quest to reduce the unemployment canker. In spite of the empirical findings that most SMEs do not survive beyond five years; **Chiedu Okonta's** book on **Keys to Sustainable SMEs** gives the reader/entrepreneur the prerequisites for his/her business to achieve sustainable growth.

There are plethora of reasons leveled to explain why businesses collapse; these include: financial challenges (from creditors and financial institutions); business environment (from investment climate); social networking (relationship with customers and suppliers). These challenges further include: prudent management/ governance systems and global competitions. Special note ought to be given to Human Resources challenges arising out of emotions, such as envy and jealousy.

Keys to Sustainable Small & Medium Enterprises is a practical book that addresses all the challenges enumerated above and would make your dream business realized, grow, and be sustained. The content of this book is as beautiful as the cover. I recommend it for all.

Nana Dr Michael Agyekum Addo

The Founder & CEO

KAMA Group/MIKADDO Holdings LTD

All Time Entrepreneur Award Winner in Ghana (EF)

REVIEW

This book, **Keys to Sustainable Small & Medium Enterprises (SMEs)** by Chiedu Okonta, addresses the financial management lapses facing SMEs in a very simplified, but impactful form. The book is not only practical-based, but also spiced with the personal experiences of the author, spanning over two decades in the financial sector.

The author has painstakingly addressed the basics of financial management in an easy to read and assimilate language with succinct practical illustrations that will be understandable to any reader, regardless of finance background.

Isaac Kweku Maison *MPHIL (Finance), ICA, ACIB, GSIC, CIMA(TOC) B.COM*

CHAPTER 1

WHY SUSTAINABLE SMEs?

A study into the economies of nations revealed that SMEs are the largest provider of world-wide employment and remained the dominant greatest contributor to each nation's GDP *(Gross Domestic Product)* over the years. GDP in a simplified form, is the total value of goods and services generated within a country in a year.

According to the World Bank Report- SMEs contribute **90%** of the world businesses and provide over **50%** of employment world - wide.

According to the Economic Indicators, SMEs contributed an average of **GBP473 million** of United Kingdom economy between 2001 and 2013.

According to the ME Financial Health; A total of **4.9million** UK businesses currently employ a total of **24.3million** workforce producing **GBP3.3 Trillion** turnovers in 2019. Out of this, **4.85million** SMEs businesses provide **19.83 million (81.6%)** of UK workforce

WASHINGTON, D.C. – Small businesses are the lifeblood of the U.S. economy: they create two-thirds **or 67%** of net new jobs and drive U.S. innovation and competitiveness. The report_shows that SMEs account for **44%** of U.S. economic activity/GDP (Gross Domestic Product). *Office for Advocacy*

CHINA: The development of **SMEs** has increasingly **contributed to China's** economic growth, which make up of over **99%** of all businesses in **China** today. The output value of **SMEs** accounts for at least **60%** of **CHINA's GDP**, generating more than **82%** of employment opportunities in **China**. OECD Library

JAPAN SMEs accounted for **70%** of national employment, compared to **60%** for the OECD area. The **SMEs** generate more than **50%** of national value added/GDP.

FRANCE SMEs make a significant **contribution** to the **French** 'non-financial business economy'. They account for **58%** of value added/GDP (Gross Domestic Product), with **61.6%** share of employment.

Apart from the SMEs sector being the backbone of major developed economies, as well as key contributors to employment, and growth of international trade, SMEs are the strongest backbone to other economies of the world, creating jobs, and innovations, and generating very significant value to national economies annually. SMEs have been adjudged the fastest catalyst for economic growth and development of nations.

In South Africa, SMEs account for **91%** of businesses, **60%** of South African work force, and contribute **52%** of total South Africa's GDP.

In Nigeria, SMEs contribute **96%** of businesses and **84%** of employment **in the country. SMEs also** account for **48%** of national GDP. (National Bureau of Statistics & PWC Survey)

According to the Nigeria Bureau of Statistics, Small and Medium scale Enterprises (SMEs) in Nigeria have contributed about **48%** of the national GDP in the last five years. With a total number of about **17.4 million,** they account for about **50%** of industrial jobs and nearly **90%** of the manufacturing sector, in terms of number of enterprises.

GHANA SMEs is critical economic driver in the country's economic growth. These SMEs account for more than **85%** of enterprises in Ghana. "**SMEs** are believed to **contribute** about 70 percent to **Ghana's Gross Domestic Product (GDP)**

CURRENT GLOBAL ATTENTION TO AFRICAN SMEs

The Africapitalism philosophy drive of HEIRS Holding Founder and Chairman: Tony Elumelu (C.O.N); and advocacies from all other global entities and personalities for more SMEs by Africans; are no doubt, speedily improving the current SME growth in Africa. Much more than ever therefore; there is an urgent need to understand the basic requirements for sustainable SMEs, in order to maximise the huge investments and sacrifices in establishing them.

World Bank Advisory: Small and Medium Enterprises (SMEs) play major roles in most economies, particularly in developing countries. SMEs account for the majority of businesses worldwide and are important contributors to job creation and global economic development. They represent about **90%** of businesses and more than **50%** of employment worldwide. Formal SMEs contribute up to **40%** of national income (GDP) in emerging economies. These numbers are significantly higher when informal SMEs are included.

SMEs that Failed to Stand the Test of Time.

According to the Small Business Administration (SBA) Office of Advocacy's 2018; **80%** of small businesses survive the first year.

However, from there the number falls sharply. Only about half of small businesses **-45% to 51%** survive beyond the five-year mark, depending on the year the business was started. Beyond that, only about one in three small businesses survive up to the 10-year mark and live to tell **the story**.

Data from the Bureau of Labour Statistics shows that approximately **20%** of new **businesses fail** during the **first** two **years** of being opened, **45%** during the **first** five **years**, and 65% during the **first 10 years**. Only **25%** of new **businesses** make it to 15 **years** or more. *(Feb 28, 2020)*

These statistics have been fairly consistent since the 1990s.

In spite of the high level of SMEs in every nation's economy and its dominant impact on every country's national income (GDP), empirical study has shown that only **25% of SMEs** survived up to 15 years and beyond. This implies that on the average, **75%** of all the SMEs Founders that commenced businesses do not have sustainable business beyond their life time! This is easily validated by taking a rough calculation of SMEs that have transformed to big corporate entities, or survived beyond 15 years from one place to another.

ABSOLUTE NEED FOR SUSTAINABLE SMEs

This is considered very serious, because the investments and efforts to commence a thriving business is much and should not be wasted without extending to the next generation! This book is thus a vital tool required to reverse that trend. It does not really matter what level one currently operates, either as an SME owner, prospective SME owner, Lecturer/Teacher, Parent, employer or government functionaries in charge of formulating economic policies that need SMEs to open the economies for growth and development, would all find this book very useful.

POST COVID -19 IMPORTANCE OF VISION

The COVID-19 epidemic which halted the economy of every nation for months; will surely have long lasting consequences on businesses going forward, and SMEs will not be excluded. The immediate mandatory outcome is that every individual, people and nations have been forced to learn self-dependence. This is contrary to the practice of globalisation and liberalisation that the world was exposed to since the second world war. It would thus cause a dramatic paradigm shift in the world economy. Some of the immediate effects are outlined below:

1. Only essential goods and services would continue to enjoy high demands
2. Examples of essential goods and services are: health care services, food and drinks products and services; and shelter
3. All goods and services in the value chain of essential goods and services shall be in high demand
4. The fact that it is an essential goods and services, or it is in the value chain may not be a total guarantee for great patronage
5. The mode of distribution has definitely been altered, because person to person contact would continue to be discouraged for at least the next two years
6. Most people and nations in order to make impact are going to strive for internal sourcing of goods and services

CHAPTER 2

Basic Foundation for any Small & Medium Establishment (SME)

Every great business in the world today started at some point as a Small or Medium Establishment. There are fundamental principles required for a solid foundation of an SME, which have been the major success factors of many businesses that have transformed from SMEs to long lasting entities. Please let us see some of these key factors:

1. **Distinguishing between the business and the owner/proprietor:** This is a process where every business decision in respect of the entity should be based absolutely on the overall best interest of the organization. This principle should apply to all areas of the business, including, but not limited to: staff recruitment, remuneration, discipline, choice of suppliers, choice of business locations, expenditure management, management of the business resources, investment decisions, pricing decisions, among others. etc. This is one of the most vital aspects of the business sustainability.

   - One of the hidden key success factors for the then Standard Trust Bank's unprecedented growth under the leadership of the then MD/CEO and currently the Group Chairman of UBA Group; Tony Elumelu **(CON)** was this factor.
   - One of the winning factors for the Living Faith World Wide Ministry's undeniable rapid growth is the clear separation between the Presiding Bishop and the Ministry itself.

Though many people are aware of this factor, not everyone can actually implement it in their businesses. This is because it requires a lot of courage, discipline and consistency to ignore the natural sentiments, emotions, and impulses associated with humans. The driving force to implement this seemingly painful factor in an entity, is the overall benefits it brings in the long run!

2. Documented Vision, Mission, & Policies:

- There must be documented clear vision and mission of the business. The Bible in **Habakuk Chapter 2:2 states: *"Write down the vision, make it clear that he who reads it can run with it!"*** It does not have to be sophisticated, at least for a start. He says "make it clear" not sophisticated. This should point everyone to the destination of the business and provide the direction or **'the how'** to get there.

- The Policies of the business are the set of rules that must guide every action, every process and every member of the business. This is quite important to eliminate subjectivity and arbitrary handling of issues. It promotes standardization and objectivity in arriving at decisions affecting every aspect of the business. The policy statement must cover every key aspect of the business, which should generally cover all Human Resources issues, Expenditure issues, key areas of the business, Accounting & Book keeping issues and Corporate Governance issues

- It should not just end at having the visions, missions and policies for the organization, but there must be clear and proper communication of such information, to all concerned. There must be deliberate attempt to enforce the implementation of the vision, missions and policies, among all the stakeholders. In particular, there should be the willingness and readiness to enforce its application at all levels, with applicable consequence management for non-compliance.

CHAPTER 3

The key product or services for the SME

- *One major aspect of your business growth is the type of product offering to your customers:* The reason we are in business is to serve and meet or surpass the need of our customers. The product or services we are dealing with determines the extent of our patronage. If we consider the residents around the North Pole, they would naturally not require refrigerators, selling of Umbrella or rain coat in the dry season would definitely lack the required patronage. It is important to bear in mind that products/services demanded at one location may differ from one location to another, and from time to time.

- *The product/service should be the type required by customers:*

  The extent to which an individual would require a product/service would depend on the extent to which he/she finds the product/service necessary for his/her existence. A 50% price reduction in a 5-star hotel services would not attract a medium/low income earner to patronize the 5-star hotel. Whereas, such individual may not change their minds if the general price levels for basic food items increase by 20%.

  The extent of changes in consumer demand for goods/services is measured in economics under Elasticity of demand. In general, the more individuals are unlikely to change their demand behaviour for a particular good/service due to changes in prices, the more INELASTIC the demand for the product/service. On the other hand, if individuals demand behaviours are more prone to changes in response to change in price of good/services, the more ELASTIC the demand for such goods/services.

  Thus the more inelastic the demand for a product/service, the more beneficial it is for the entrepreneur and vice versa.

Applying the principle of Maslow's Hierarchy of Needs, the products and services that meet the basic needs of the society have proven to be the goods/services with higher INELASTICITY, which implies that the consumers would keep demanding for them irrespective of slight changes in prices. This includes the goods/services that meet the physiological needs of man, such as food, shelter, water and air.

There is a myth that needs to be conquered here. That is that customers would naturally like what the seller has passion for. I found out that is not necessarily true. Can you imagine a professional footballer who insists that since he loves football, the only business he can do is selling of football? Obviously he would soon realize how unrealistic that can be! **Whatever products or services we are selling must be the ones the customers within our coverage area are prepared to buy and pay for on demand.**

- ***Non- seasonal products/services are preferred by customers***

    Every entrepreneur should strive to stick to goods /services that are required by consumers throughout the year. This is different from seasonal products/services. This is very important as the capacity for generating the seasonal products/services may become latent within the year, which increases the cost of business and ultimately reduces the business income generation.

    The more customers that can be reached and the longer the coverage across the year, the better for the business entity in generating business wealth.

- ***It should be products/services that attract more customers***

    No matter how basic or sophisticated any product/service is, it is meant for a certain category of customers, who would actually need the product/services. The SME should ensure the product/service is suited to meet the need of its target market.

For example, the selling of milk was at a time packaged to meet the needs of the premium class, but the premium class was made up of many adults and aged members of the society, who did not need milk. Hence, currently, the selling of milk has largely been packaged to suit the various categories of customers that really need milk. It is the major duty of the SME to ensure the products/services are packaged in suitable quantities and delivered to the customers that need them, at the various locations and quantities they are needed, and at the right times.

- ***It should be a product/service people buy and pay for immediately***

The extent of the demand elasticity as described above would determine to what extent customers would be prepared to part with their money to acquire those goods/services. Some customers would prefer to even pay in advance for certain products/services, while the same set of customers may consider buying other products/services only if better conditions, such as price discounts, quantity discounts and credit sales are provided. All these sales conditions have negative impact on the business income generation. It is most advised that business entrepreneurs deal in products/services that attract immediate cash payments for their sales.

- ***Finally, it is better to have a product that attracts more customers than you can serve!***

Competition can involve a lot of intrigues that could be very costly for any organization. In order to reduce the cost of advertisement or the cost of competition, the entrepreneur, as much as possible, should strive to deal in products/services that have ready customer base anywhere and anytime. This is better than having a product/service that would force the SME to be at the mercy of customers.

The SME must Build Competitive Edge for its Product/Service

It does not matter how much a product or service is demanded by customers; in order to ensure sustainable growth, the SME should ensure in-built competitive advantage for its product/service. This is a process whereby the SME distinguishes its product/service offerings by providing excellent and superior customer services with personalized touch. The competitive edge can further be created by the SME that employs technological knowhow or installations to distinguish its service offerings from others.

CHAPTER 4
Fundamental principles of accounting

One of the essential requirements necessary for the Small and Medium scale Enterprise (SME) to be solidly established for sustainable growth, is the recognition of the fundamental principle of accounting from the onset. This is very important; because what gets measured gets done. The fundamental principle of accounting implies that every financial transaction must be duly recorded with a credit entry and a corresponding debit entry. The word "corresponding" here, means that it is the same transaction showing the same amount, narration, date, and transaction ID and it is duly captured in both debit and credit records of the SME.

DAILY ACCOUNTING SUMMARY

At the end of each day, each month, and year, the total of debit entries shall be same as the total of credit entries. The core duty of Accounting, which includes: recording, classifying, summarizing, analyzing and interpreting financial records for effective management decision making; is vital for the SME's sustainable growth. It is thus highly advised that from the onset the services of an Accountant should be sought to directly/remotely ensure the standard accounting records are maintained for the SME. There should be documented records of the business daily, monthly and yearly performances, which are necessary ingredients for quality business decisions

One of the first SMEs we supervised was an electronics Trading company at Alaba International Market, Ojo Alaba, Lagos State Nigeria, which started on a small scale in 1999. But as at 2004, based on implementation of the various guidelines we provided, the company had grown into a bigger entity with several branches, and till date, the company has been solidly established as a sustainable entity.

Since then till date, we have had to provide background financial management services to several SMEs, ranging from establishment guidelines in form of sound business proposals to financial management services, that put the companies on their paths for sustainable growth. The financial management services generally assist the companies to harness their business potentials and eliminate wastes and losses at various levels, resulting in the achievement of sustainable progress in their businesses.

Excellent handling of Human Resources

To achieve a sustainable business growth in particular, and sustainability as a whole; there must be conscious efforts to ensure objective handling of all Human Resources issues. This is due to the critical position of Human Resources in accomplishing every organizational success, growth, and sustainability. The crucial functions of Human Resources that must be handled effectively and objectively include:

- Recruitment,
- Compensation,
- Welfare, and Training
- Performance Management and
- Disciplinary Process

EFFECTIVE HANDLING OF HUMAN RESOURCES ISSUES:

The **Singapore Prime Minister (Lee Kuan Yew)** narrating the secret behind the aggressive transformation of Singapore from a 3rd World country to a 1st World country within two decades explained, it was mainly due to **"meritocracy"**. This is the process of ensuring that the right person with cognate experience and qualifications is selected for every assignment; irrespective of all other sentimental conditions.

As a follow up to the principle of meritocracy, every business that expects to succeed and enjoy sustainable growth should ensure fair and commensurate compensation and treatment is meted to each staff according to their respective **contributions** and qualifications.

PERFORMANCE EVALUATION

Effective management of the entity's Human resources should also include proper and objective assessment of each staff performance. This should be done periodically, say bi annually and the outcome of every performance evaluation should result in business decisions that aptly recognize and reward excellent performers, while non performers should be disciplined accordingly.

ABILITY TO FIRE AS AND WHEN NEEDED

A very crucial aspect of Human Resources function is the ability to recognize when to discipline and fire any defaulting employee. This is an inevitable decision, every business owner must know when and how to take. It must not be done out of sentiments, nor process of eliminating perceived enemies. Rather it should be in accordance with the entity's established Human Resources Process and Disciplinary policy; for which the confirmed offenders should be treated accordingly.

SUCCESSION PLAN

One of the major causes of business collapse of well-established SMEs is lack of conscious efforts to nurture and set the necessary guidelines for business succession. As it is said; **Today is the Tomorrow we were looking for Yesterday!** Hence every SME needs to; as a matter of urgency Today; set the necessary guideline for its business succession Tomorrow! This should be followed with deliberate efforts to nurture next generation; by providing the relevant education and practical training, that should sufficiently equip the prospective business successors to meet the challenges of

Tomorrow! Successful management of any business is an art that must be learnt and imbibed more from practice than in theory.

Every business owner and indeed nation, should incorporate the right Human Resources practices of meritocracy, objectivity, and result oriented leadership in order to realize its goals and sustain its business growth.

CHAPTER 5

The SME Income and Expenditure Account

A very crucial record of every SME is the Income and Expenditure account. This is the account that captures every cost of making and selling the products/services from production stage to after sales services. It equally captures every income line from sales proceeds to all fees. The typical Income & Expenditure account can be enumerated as below:

INCOME AND EXPENDITURE ACCOUNT FOR THE YEAR ENDED DECEMBER 31ST 2019

EXPENDITURES	USD	INCOME	USD
Used Materials	XXX	Sales proceeds	XXX
Cost of sales	XXX	Fees Received	XXX
Salaries & Wages	XXX	Rent Received	XXX
Discounts granted	XXX	Discount Received	XXX
Rent Expenses	XXX	Interests Received	XXX
Telephone & Comm	XXX	Dividend Received	XXX
Electricity expenses	XXX	Profit from sale of Assets	XXX
Insurance cost	XXX	Other incomes	XXX
Audit & Professional	XXX		
Repairs & Maintenance	XXX	**Deficits**	XXX
Depreciation	XXX		
Entertainment cost	XXX		
Transport cost	XXX		
SURPLUS	XXX		
TOTAL Expenses/Income XXX		Total Income/Expenses	XXX

NOTE:

The above table which captures all the expenses on the Left Hand Side **(LHS)** of the table and all income of the SMEs on the Right Hand Side **(RHS)** of the table is meant to have the same total figure.

If the incomes on the RHS exceeds the expenses *(which is expected in business anyway)*, the difference should be captured as surplus amount on the LHS, in which case the total on both sides becomes, **the total of income.** In the unlikely event that the expenses exceed the income, then the difference should be **'Deficits'** to be captured on the RHS as the balancing figure, while the total amount on both sides becomes the **Total Expenses.**

APPROPRIATION OF INCOME

Every SME that would attain sustainable growth need to develop the required discipline and knowledge on how to appropriate the surplus/income generated from its business on monthly and yearly basis. The following general rules may be applied:

1. For every **$100** surplus generated from the business after taxation, at least **$30** should be devoted to the business. This is necessary to continuously grow capacity that would keep the SME having competitive advantage over its rival entities.

2. It is recommended that any drawing from the surplus should be strictly in line with the Dividend policy of the company, say **10% or 15%** of the SME annual surplus should be used for dividend payment

4. For every surplus of **$100**, it is advised that **$30** should be devoted to Research and Development as well as structural development of the SME. This is quite necessary in order to build more capacity for future productivity, thereby boosting its competitive edge.

CHAPTER 6:
6.0. The SME Balance Sheet

The Balance sheet should provide the SME the financial statement of its affairs; showing own resources and exposures/obligations at every point in time. This is the statement showing the amount invested by the entrepreneurs, plus every other fund lent to the SME on one side and the SME own resources used in creating value for the SME on the other hand.

6.1 SME BALANCE SHEET AS AT ………..

DESCRIPTION	2019	2018	2017	2016	2015
ASSETS	USD	USD	USD	USD	USD
CASH	XXX	XXX	XXX	XXX	XXX
BANK	XXX	XXX	XXX	XXX	XXX
Short term securities	XXX	XXX	XXX	XXX	XXX
Debtors	XXX	XXX	XXX	XXX	XXX
Stock	XXX	XXX	XXX	XXX	XXX
Total Current Assets	**XXX**	**XXX**	**XXX**	**XXX**	**XXX**
Fixed Assets					
Motor Vehicles	XXX	XXX	XXX	XXX	XXX
Plant & Machinery	XXX	XXX	XXX	XXX	XXX
Furniture & Fittings	XXX	XXX	XXX	XXX	XXX
Land & Buildings	XXX	XXX	XXX	XXX	XXX
Total Assets	**XXX**	**XXX**	**XXX**	**XXX**	**XXX**
Liability					
Accrued Expenses	XXX	XXX	XXX	XXX	XXX
Short term Loans	XXX	XXX	XXX	XXX	XXX
Over Drafts	XXX	XXX	XXX	XXX	XXX
Total Current Liability	**XXX**	**XXX**	**XXX**	**XXX**	**XXX**
Long term loans	XXX	XXX	XXX	XXX	XXX
Debentures	XXX	XXX	XXX	XXX	XXX
Shareholders Reserves	**XXX**	**XXX**	**XXX**	**XXX**	**XXX**
Capital Invested	XXX	XXX	XXX	XXX	XXX
Total Liabilities	**XXX**	**XXX**	**XXX**	**XXX**	**XXX**

Key to Sustainable SME by Chiedu Okonta

5.2 RELATIONSHIP BETWEEN THE BALANCE SHEET AND THE INCOME STATEMENT

The interesting relationship between the SME Balance Sheet and its Income and Expenditure account, is that the business **income surplus or (deficit)** from the Income and Expenditure account would be added/(deducted) from the SME's periodic Reserve. In effect, the greater the surplus, the more the SME Balance Sheet is growing and vice versa.

What Happens if the Balance Sheet Does not Balance?

It was explained in section 6.0 above that the total of Assets would be the same as the total of Liability and capital. This appears very simplified, but a typical Small and Medium scale business would not always have the total Assets and total Liability balances agree. The major cause of the imbalance is usually caused by single entries as against the standard accounting practice of double entry system. Some SMEs have the practice of ignoring the double entry system, thus maintaining only single entry system. In order to correct imbalances in the balance sheet, the outstanding items should be identified and be properly posted to conform with the double entry principle

The best practice should be that every financial transaction should be accompanied with a double entry posting in two separate accounts; with a debit entry and a corresponding credit entry in another account.

At the end of each day, or month, or year, the balances in each account is used to prepare the balance sheet, which should have equal total assets and total liabilities.

CHAPTER 7:

Effective Management of the Assets

The SME's owned assets are expected to generate value for the SME, but poor management of the assets could result in losses, rather than value addition. Every item in the SME assets should actually generate value for the SME, else, they are value 'eroders', and would ultimately bring down the entity, if the trend is not reversed. Below are tips on how you can ensure each asset of the company is generating value for the SME:

1. **CASH & BANK BALANCES**

   The cash held in hand and/or Petty Cash balances of an SME or the cash held in vault by a financial institution, are needed to the extent that they are necessary to meet the urgent/daily cash needs of the company. It is required that careful study or assessment should be done to ascertain the necessary cash limit for every SME at any point in time, beyond which the cash of the entity should be invested in income yielding assets, like Call deposit or other fixed term deposits.

   The SME must have a culture that every cash and sales proceeds generated by the SME; should be fully and promptly lodged into the Bank account of the SME, from where the approved cash limit/Petty Cash should be withdrawn for the SME's official utilization. Keeping cash that is not immediately required by the SME can be compared to the Prodigal son that collected the cash worth of his wealth, and departed into the unknown, where he wasted all his wealth in riotous living. The practice of any SME keeping cash for which there is no immediate need should be avoided at all times.

   Effective use of the Digital banking products would further enhance the cash management system, which reduces/eliminates the associated risks in holding cash.

The more settlements are done online via the Digital banking channels, the less dependence on physical cash payments, thereby eliminating the risks of cash pilferage, shortages and other holding costs.

The SME that has various bank accounts and banking activities must demand for monthly bank reconciliation statements and have a policy that ensures all outstanding bank transactions are **resolved within maximum of five (5) working days.** By so doing, the SME would be getting increased value from its banking activities.

2. SHORT TERM SECURITIES

For every SME that is capable of generating short term funding different from the normal income lines, such funds should be promptly invested in short term securities such as monthly Call/Fixed Deposits, Treasury Bills etc. Other SME are characteristically designed to generate large cash. It is recommended that such excess cash should be promptly invested in short term securities once they are generated.

3. DEBTORS

This is one area an SME can easily lose value; if proper attention is not paid to it, because it is a non-income yielding asset. It is a situation where the SME has sold its goods/services on credit. From Chapter two, we understand that this type of asset occurs more for SMEs dealing with elastic goods/services. Notwithstanding, some companies would still have Debtors, if it helps to increase sales volume and the credit customers have the right character and capacity to pay up promptly. The SME should have clear policies or guidelines that show how to handle credit sales. Once an SME has taken a decision to sell its goods/services to customers on credit, the following process may be adopted:

i. **Sales Discount:** Sales Discount is used to effectively manage credit sales. This is a situation where the SME uses discount to woo its customers to pay promptly. For example, **10%** discount for cash sales, **5%** discount for cash payment within 10 days and 0% discount for 30 days' credit sales.

ii. In some instances, the discount days may spread up to 60 days or 90 days. It is instructive to note that the higher the days of discounts, the higher the chances of credit default. There is usually a default risk attached to every discount sale. It is thus very important to have properly analyzed the character and capacity profile of every customer that buys on credit. The company should have standard letter of agreement between the SME and the credit customer, which should have clearly defined rules of engagements that incorporate the inherent risks in the credit sales in the best interest of the SME.

iii. It is important to ensure there is adequate record of debtors and that the debtors are followed up with relevant prompts to settle their balances on time. There should be consequence managements for debtors that fail to settle their obligations as and when due. This may include cancelation of credit sales services to such customers and many more.

4. STOCK

The stock here typically refers to the value of goods being sold by the SME, which are yet to be sold. This is another aspect of non-income yielding asset. Thus the lower the value of stock, the better for the SME, and most importantly; the shorter the stock cycle for the SME, the better it is for the SME. The stock cycle is the average period it takes the goods/services to be produced/bought and sold to the customers either via cash or credit sales.

Accountants have several methods of treating stock, depending on the nature of goods/services being sold.

FIRST IN FIRST OUT (FIFO): This method assumes that the goods that were bought first should be the first to be sold. Hence at the end of the year, the available goods should be the most recent stock of goods purchased. Considering that in general terms, selling prices rise with time, it is usually believed that the recent stock will be at higher prices compared to the goods bought and sold earlier in the year. The major impact this has for Accountants is that the closing value of stock would be relatively higher than the value of stock at the earlier part of the year, which would result in overstatement of profit for the SME in the real sense of it.

LAST IN LAST FIRST OUT (LIFO): Unlike FIFO, the LIFO method of valuing stock implies that goods that were bought last should be the first to be sold. As such, at the end of the year, the available goods should be the most previous stock of goods purchased. Using the FIFO analysis above, all things being equal, **LIFO tend to** address the concern noted from **FIFO** method. However, LIFO method leaves a challenge that if we allow the goods that came in last to be sold first, stock items may become spoilt in the process, obsolete, dilapidated or even pilfered; which would erode more value for the SME.

WEIGHTED AVERAGE METHOD: In order to solve the concerns created by FIFO and LIFO method, Accountants developed the use of Weighted average cost of goods. This is simply taking all the available goods in terms of price per unit and corresponding value, then arrive at weighted average stock value at a time. For example, assuming an SME with a mono product buys its goods once in a month throughout the year:

DESCRIPTION	Quantity	Price/Unit $	Total $
January total purchases	120	5.00	600
February total purchases	200	5.00	1,000
March total purchases	180	5.10	918
April total purchases	180	5.10	918
May total purchases	200	5.20	1,040
June total purchase	160	5.20	832
July total purchases	200	5.25	1,050
August total purchases	200	5.25	1,050
September total purchases	190	5.30	1,007
October total purchases	150	5.40	810
November total purchases	170	5.40	918
December total purchases	120	5.40	648
TOTAL	2,070	62.60	10,791
WEIGHTED AVERAGE (10,791/2,070)		5.21	

Thus a more scientific means of arriving at the closing stock is the weighted average unit price of **$5.21**; which was arrived at by adding up all the value of stock purchased throughout the year and dividing it by the total quantity of goods bought. The closing stock is thus arrived at by multiplying the quantity of closing stock, (say 300 units) by the weighted average price, which becomes **$1,563**

Building Assets in Shares: Another form of stock is building assets in shares. Any SME that generates high liquidity in an organized economy with price stability and low inflation rate may invest in shares. ***This must be based only on a well-informed decision that the nation's economy is progressive and the company being invested in; is progressive and has good products/services, good customers' demand, strong management structure and pedigree of dividend payment.***

CAUTION! CAUTION!! CAUTION!!!

There is need for caution in taking decisions to invest in shares. This is in spite of the good benefits from investment in shares from share appreciation to annual dividend payments. These potential benefits have deceived so many people in the past to ignorantly invest huge sums of money in shares, without understanding the underlying fundamentals.

In Nigeria for example, post 2004, after the **Professor Charles Soludo** led Banking Capitalization that compelled every commercial bank in the country to have minimum paid up share capital increased from (Two to Twenty-Five) Billion (NGN2 to NGN25) Billion; all the commercial banks, most of which were not publicly quoted then, had to resort to the capital market in order to fully comply with the regulatory minimum paid up share capital requirement. This attracted several Foreign Direct Investments **(FDI)**, who were targeting short term gains from the nation's capital market. As a result, the prices of several stocks increased rapidly within a short time, but the total market capitalization **(NGN24Trillion)** then could not be reasonably substantiated by underlying fundamentals.

In 2008 in response to the 2007 Global financial failure, most of the FDI, suddenly withdrew their investments from Nigerian Stock Market, resulting in drastic drop in the nation's stock market capitalization from **NGN24 trillion to NGN4.2 Trillion.** That sharp decrease of about **NGN20Trillion** was the wealth of local investors, who were mostly the vibrant working class, and local businesses, which were lost to the stock market crisis. The bitter learning points is that *nobody should jump into any new investment except you properly understand it, you have control over what happens in the business, and you are involved in the investment.*

Effective utilization of short term assets are very great avenues of generating wealth for every entity

5. **EFFECTIVE MANAGEMENT OF FIXED ASSETS:** The general rule concerning management of SME fixed assets, especially **[MOTOR VEHICLES, FIXTURES AND FITTINGS and PLANT & MACHINERY]**, is to ensure you do not invest in any of them until the business actually requires it. Once it is established that the SME's business needs the fixed assets, then the SME should strive to buy the actual fixed asset required that should suit the need of the SME. For example, where a Bus is required, there is no point buying a jeep instead, and if outsourcing Plant & Machinery at the initial stage, or using hire purchase is better, then, let it be done! Whatever amount is invested in these fixed assets, it should only make the company to generate more wealth and not to suffocate the SME.

6. **BUILDINGS & LAND:** This aspect has been reserved till the end of this session, because of its obvious uniqueness and importance. Real Sustainable growth of an SME cannot be achieved without a conscious effort to grow real estates at every available opportunity. In spite of the delicate nature of real estates and the risks associated with acquiring it, this remains an inevitable source of sustainable growth.

For example, a property around Amuwo area of Lagos-Nigeria, which was priced at **NGN3.2 million/USD25,200** in 2007, but in 2012 the same property was on sale for **NGN20 Million/USD133,3333**. The following tips about land and buildings acquisition may be useful:

i) **Acquisition of land and buildings must be subjected to prior due diligence and extended due diligence** involving the experts such as: Lawyers, Surveyors, Architects, Builders etc. You would always appreciate the discipline that every of your decision to buy or sell real estate, is based on recommendation from your experts.

ii) As much as it is practicable, it is far better to own your office building than to rent it. We would always support the idea of not overloading the business with expenses of fixed assets, but with proper planning, the financing of land and building creation, can be seamlessly done without overburdening the business with immediate financial outlay.

iii) Developing areas have the high tendency to grow. Identifying such areas ahead of time and investing in land and building at such locations ahead of the development may just open up great opportunity. *"President Donald Trump- Real Estate 101"*

iv) The value of your investments in suitable land and building is of great importance to a lot of your stakeholders including: bankers, investors, government, tax authorities and customers. The financial losses an SME incurs every year for operating without suitable land and building is unquantifiable!

ADVANTAGES OF OWNING LAND & BUILDING

The following are the immediate examples of benefits for an SME that owns its land and buildings:

(i) **Overall Less Expensive Compared to Rent:** The cumulative rent the SME would pay for five years of using the property could buy the property.

(ii) **Tax Benefits:** The SME that occupies its own property would eliminate the rent expense and in addition gain capital allowance, which indirectly make the building cost a tax deductible expense.

(iii) **Other Benefits**: Any SME that operates in its own property is capable of enjoying **(1)** more liquidity over the useful part of the asset; as the cost that should have been incurred on rent payment is conserved. Other benefits of land and building include: **(2)** the associated prestige, **(3)** increased credibility; since it could be used as collateral to access banking facility, and **(4)** capital appreciation as the property increases in value.

CHAPTER 8:

Effective Management of the Liabilities

Liabilities are generally the obligations of the company to outsiders including its creditors and owners. The below section seeks to highlight the key benefits from effective management of the SMEs liability profile:

Short term loans & Overdrafts

Short term liabilities are those obligations of the SME to its creditors that would fall due within a year. They include but not limited to the following: Accrued expenses; Accounts Payable; Overdrafts and other short term loans:

i) **Accrued Expenses:** This is a situation where the suppliers or contractors of an SME allow the company to receive goods/services and pay at a future date. It is a form of financing at zero interest rate; therefore, it is highly recommended, provided the proceeds is in respect of the SME's business, for which there is a ready market.

ii) **Overdrafts and other short term loans:** This is a form of liability where an SME borrows from a bank or other sources to finance its short term business activity. There is usually a cost in terms of interest attached to this liability. It is not advisable for an SME to accept this liability; except the business annual return on investment is at least twice the cost of borrowing and the amount borrowed can be repaid within the business cash circle. ***Please see Chapters nine and twelve***

iii) **Accounts Payables:** These are the financial obligations of the company to its suppliers, service providers, and contractors, for which their payments are provided for till the agreed time of payment. These provisions are usually represented in Balance Sheet as Accounts Payable under Liabilities.

Given that the business activity is progressive and viable, SMEs are encouraged to extend the time of paying for the Accounts Payable. For example, if the SME has the policy to pay its Accounts Payable 30 or 60 or 90 days after the goods are delivered or services rendered, then such fund would boost working capital during that period. This is preferable; provided the credit worthiness of the SME is not affected.

CHAPTER 9:
Making the best from banking loans

Many companies have witnessed tremendous growth within a short span of time due to utilization of banking loans; while some other companies have crashed due to their utilization of banking loans. It is therefore very important to know those factors necessary for successful utilization of banking loans.

Who Qualifies to Borrow?

Scripturally, we understand the mind of God concerning borrowing. Every child of God is mandated not to borrow **(Deut 15:6; 28:12 &13 and Prov. 22:7).** *This is because the borrower is a slave to the lender.* As an individual, one is not expected to borrow in order to finance personal lifestyle, such as financing feeding, or dressing, or payment for transport costs; or payment for rent or payment for school fees or to organize party.

However, we saw in two instances where God commanded his children to borrow **(Exodus 11:2 & 3 and 12: 35 & 36)** jewels of silver, jewels of gold & jewels of clothes. Also in **2Kings4:3** God commanded that: *'not a few empty vessels should be borrowed'.* But in **verse 7,** he said: *'sell the oil and pay off the debt'.* The two instances where God allowed his children to borrow, both were business related. The Egyptians one way or the other; had to settle the Israelites for their years of hard labour, while the oil was sold and the proceeds used to pay for the outstanding debt; including the cost of borrowing the empty vessels!

It is therefore clear that God does not want his children to live under the burden of debt, but a business entity, with a thriving business may borrow, purely for business, provided the business entity can satisfy the below conditions:

i) The business entity that must borrow should be sure that the yearly return on investment for that company is at least twice the total cost of borrowing the loan. Annual return on investment is the profit of the company after paying all the expenses including tax; divided by shareholders' fund. The shareholders fund is the capital invested plus the retained profit or Reserve. The total cost of loan is the interest rate plus all other charges.

ii) For example: An SME made profit after tax of **USD100,000** in 2019. If the capital invested is **USD150,000** and the Reserve is **50,000.** Then, the Return on Investment should be USD100,000/USD200,000, which is **50%**. If the interest rate is 20% and other charges is 3%, then the total cost of borrowing is **23%**. For this SME to be able to repay its debt, the SME Return on Investment, which is **50%** must be at least twice the total cost of borrowing, which is **23%** here. So this company may take the overdraft.

iii) **Source of Repayment:** The next area to consider before taking a banking loan is the SME source of repayment. This is so vital, because banking loan is not a gratuity, but an obligation that must be settled. The source of repayment must be from the business being financed. If the business being financed generates inflows in 90 days and above, then it is wrong to obtain a banking loan with 30 days' maturity period.

iv) The SME that must borrow should ensure its source of repayment comes earlier than the maturity period of the facility obtained. This has great advantage of ensuring that default interest is not applied, if the facility becomes unpaid at maturity. Besides, an SME that has consistent record of clearing its loan on or before maturity, secures credibility from the Bank, which would assist the SME in future financing.

CHAPTER 10

OPTIMAL HANDLING OF TAXATION ISSUES

Optimal Handling of Taxation Issues for SMEs

An SME that should have a sustainable growth should have a financial policy that takes advantage of the existing tax laws to derive some tax benefits in the overall interest of the SME. This is not an illegality at all, as we encourage all our clients to be compliant with each tax laws. Notwithstanding, it is highly recommended that the SME, may either have a Tax Adviser or handle it directly, by ensuring that every available tax advantage is taken to reduce its tax liability.

1. **Taxation of SMEs in Ghana**
    The main laws that regulate corporate/income taxation in Ghana for example; are the Income Tax Act 2015, (**Act 896**) and its amendments; and the Income Tax Regulations, 2016 (**L.I 2244**). General corporate tax rate is **25%** (**35%** for companies into mining and petroleum). The practice is not significantly different in other nations like Nigeria and South Africa

2. **How to Obtain Tax Advantages for an SME?**
- **Type of Entity to Register:** Companies are taxed separately from the shareholders. SMEs registered as companies generally pay **25%** (and **35%** if into mining or petroleum). The shareholders also pay additional **8%** on their dividends. However, for SMEs registered as sole proprietorships, the business is not taxed separately; only the sole proprietor pays PAYE tax, at a graduated rate currently ranging from **NIL** to **30%** (if income exceeds **GHS240,000** per annum).

- **Business Location:** An SME manufacturing company located in **Accra or Tema** pays full **25%** corporate tax; while those located in **other regional capitals** pay **18.75%** corporate tax; while those located **outside the Regional capitals**, pay only **12.5%** corporate tax

In Nigeria, SMEs cited outside the State Capitals and Federal Capital Territory enjoy tax rebates, while SMEs in Agriculture have three years' tax exemptions.

- **Nature of business/activities:** SMEs principally engaged in the **hotel industry** pay **22% tax**. Income of company engaged in the **export of non-traditional goods** is taxed at **8%** etc.

- **Financing Decisions:** SMEs financed with both debt/loans and equity will pay lesser tax than those financed entirely with equity. This is because interest on loan (which is tax deductible) reduces taxable income.

- **Capital Budgeting:** Capital allowance *(which is the permissible allowance for SME Fixed Assets expenditures)* in a particular year of assessment cannot be deferred. Thus capital allowance becomes irrelevant in the year if an SME makes a loss. **Good capital budgeting will ensure that fixed assets are acquired in years of high profits, so as to reduce the taxable profits.** Gains from sale of capital assets can be used to buy another asset of the same class, so as to avoid capital gains tax.

- **Recruitment policies:** SMEs that recruit **fresh graduates** from a **recognised Ghanaian tertiary institutions** are entitled to additional deductions for salary and wages paid during the year to the fresh graduates, as below:

No.	% of Fresh Graduates In Workforce	Additional Deduction
1	Up to 1%	10% of salaries and wages
2	Above 1% but not more than 5%	30% of salaries and wages
3	Above 5%	50% of salaries and wages

- **Payroll administration:** Efficient management of payroll items can reduce/avoid taxes. Overtime payments to **qualifying junior employees** (whose income does not exceed **GHS1,500** per month) are taxed at **5%** if the overtime does not exceed

50% of the basic salary, **excess overtime** is taxed at **10%**. Bonus not exceeding **15%** of annual basic salary of employee, is taxed at **5%**. Provision of accommodation by an SMEs in timber, mining, building, construction, farming business or petroleum operations to employees at site of operation is tax free.

3. Relevant tax exemptions to claim

- An SME may deduct all expenses **wholly, reasonably, exclusively** and **necessarily** incurred in the production of income, including foreign exchange losses (other than those of a capital nature); interest/finance cost; repairs and improvement costs; and **research and development expenses.**

- **Unrelieved losses** of SMEs in the following **priority sectors: (a)** Mineral/mining **(b)** Petroleum **(c)** Energy and power **(d)** Manufacturing **(e)** Agro processing **(g)** Tourism business **(h)** ICT business can be carried forward for **five years**.

- **Unrelieved losses** of companies in **all other sectors** can be carried forward against any taxable profit for **three years**.

- **Capital allowance**: This is granted IRO **depreciable asset owned** and **used** by an SME during a year of assessment in the production of business income.

- **Contributions and donations** made for a worthwhile cause and **approved by the Government** including: **(a)** contributions to charitable organization **(b)** contribution to a scholarship scheme **(c)** contribution to rural/urban area development **(d)** contribution to sports development /promotion; and any other approved worthwhile ventures is fully deductible.

- **Social Security Contributions** up to a maximum of **29.5%** by an SME (employer) to its employee are exempt from tax. Employees contribution of **5.5%** are also tax exempt.

4. **Ways to ensure reduced/or no tax payment by an SME**
   - SMEs in the following sectors enjoy concessional corporate tax rates:

Business Activity	Years	Tax Rate
Agro processing business	5 years	1%
Cocoa- by product business	5 years	1%
Certified low cost housing	5 years	1%
Tree crop farming e.g. coffee	10 years	1%
Cash crops or livestock (excluding cattle)	5 years	1%
Cattle ranching	10 years	1%
Waste processing business	7 years	1%

   - Income of a **young entrepreneur (35 years and below)** from the business of Manufacturing, ICT, Agro processing, Energy production, Waste processing, Tourism and Creative Arts, Horticulture and Medicinal plants shall be **exempt from tax for five years.** After the 5 years, the young entrepreneur will enjoy reduced taxes based on the location of the enterprise as follow: **(a)** Accra & Tema – **15%** (b) the Northern Regions – **5%** (c) other Regional capitals – **12.5%** and other areas – **10%**.

- Income of SMEs from cocoa farming is not taxable.

- SMEs registered as **Free Zone Enterprise** will pay **0%** tax for the **10 years** in operation. **After 10 years** in operation, they will pay tax at **15%** (on export).

5. Ways to ensure every tax paid is passed on to another person/entity

- VAT registered SMEs may recover their input VAT from GRA.

- Proper documentation of accounting records would enhance good pricing policies that would incorporate taxes paid as part of goods/services costs.

- Non-VAT registered SMEs and SMEs on the **3%** VAT Flat Scheme cannot recover input VAT, but they can pass on the input VAT to their customers through their pricing policies. Corporate income taxes paid by SMEs cannot be passed to customers.

6. Other Ways of Getting Tax Benefits from Tax Authority

- SMEs must collect withholding tax certificates from withholding tax agents. So that same can be reclaimed from Ghana Revenue Authority when filing tax returns.

- Withholding taxes negatively affect cash flows and working capital management. SMEs may apply to GRA for withholding taxes exemption. In practice, the Tax Authorities are very considerate in favour of SMEs when attending to this kind of application

- A resident SME business (other than a partnership) may claim a foreign tax credit for any income tax paid to a foreign country.

7. Benefits to SME for Complying with Tax Obligations

- Tax compliance helps SMEs to avoid unnecessary fines and penalties from the revenue authorities.

- Tax compliance increases business opportunities and growth. Most companies prefer to deal with SMEs that are tax compliant. Government institutions award contracts to only tax compliant SMEs.

- Tax compliance is the only way SMEs can enjoy incentives from GRA such as exemption from withholding taxes.

- Tax compliant SMEs are in the best position to attract better investors and enjoy better public visibility and acceptance.

TAX BENEFITS FROM OTHER NATIONS

Though we used the Ghanaian Tax laws as an example, the tax benefits would generally apply to every SME, irrespective of geographical location, because tax laws are usually similar and may differ only in levels. The Ghanaian tax law is one of the most developed tax laws in Sub Saharan Africa, which would give the SMEs from other geographies in Sub Saharan African nations, even greater tax benefits.

All in all, the SMEs are better positioned to receive more tax benefits/claims than an employee. Hence it is advisable for every employee to think entrepreneurship also

CHAPTER 11

Cash flow analysis

Here, we are going to see the simple definition and application of **Cash Flow Analysis** as it affects the SME, which is different from the complex technical details of this topic. Cash flow analysis is the fundamental basis that tests our understanding of building sustainable SMEs. Our knowledge from Chapters **(5)** *(Income & Expenditure account)* & **(7)** *(Effective Management of SMEs Assets)* above would enhance our quick understanding of this topic. This is so important; as many have wondered how come a company with glaring activities and evidence of good fixed assets could become bankrupt overnight?

Cash flow analysis is designed to obtain the net cash generated from the business activity of an organization within a period. There are three major components of Cash flow analysis that make up the net cash generated from the business activity, which include:

1. Cash generated from operating activities
2. Cash generated from investing activities
3. Cash generated from financing activities
4. The summation of the above is the net cash from business activity within a period
5. Number (4) is added to the opening cash balance to arrive at the closing cash balance

CALCULATION OF THE CASH FLOW ANALYSIS

The process considers the incremental cash movements between the two selected periods, and the cash movements could be negative or positive. It would be positive, if the movement results in bringing cash into the business and negative if the movement takes cash out of the business.

(i). Cash generated from operating activities: In order to know the cash generated from operating activity; we start with the SURPLUS or PBT of the company. Then add back depreciation, as depreciation, which ordinarily forms part of the business expense in income statement is not recognized as a cash inflow or outflow, this is **because depreciation does not result in cash movement.** Next we take the incremental cash movements in the working capital, which are cash movements in Current Assets and Current Liabilities.

(ii). For example:

An SME which commenced its 2019 financial year with **USD55,000** cash and cash equivalent and closed the year with **USD90,000** cash and cash equivalent; made annual **PBT/SURPLUS USD250,000**; after charging depreciation of **USD10,000**. Within the year Accrued expenses grew by **USD5,000,** Account Payable increased by **USD10,000,** Overdraft facility of **USD30,000** was fully paid off. The SME also increased its debtors balance and stock of goods balance by **USD10,000** each.

Using the above information, the Cash generated from operating activity would be calculated as follows:

	USD
The SME 2019 PBT was	250,000
Add: Depreciation	10,000
Accrued Expenses	5,000
Account payable	10,000
Less: Bank O/D paid	(30,000)
Debtors increased by	(10,000)
Stock of goods increased by	(10,000)
Cash Generated from Operating Activity	**225,000**

(iii). Cash generated from investing activity takes into consideration what the business did within the period, in terms of its fixed assets. Were there acquisitions or sale of fixed assets? Were there other investments the SME undertook within the period or not? Noting in all cases, that what is at stake here is the incremental cash increase or decrease from all the investment decisions. Still using the example of the above SME, assuming the company executed the following capital expenditure within 2019: Bought more Plant & Machinery worth **USD40,000,** bought more Land & Building worth **USD100,000.** Increased its shareholding in another SME worth **USD10,000**

The SME cash generated from investing activity would be as follows:

	USD
Plant & Machinery	40,000
Land & Building	100,000
Increased investment in XYZ Ltd	10,000
Cash Generated from Investing Activity:	**(150,000)**

(iv). Cash generated from financing activities: Here we are considering cash from financing activity, which include long term financing by owners or creditors, or suppliers. The incremental cash from the financing activity could be positive or negative, depending on whether the cash is coming in or going out of the business. Still using our above example, supposing the SME received dividend worth of **USD5,000** from its subsidiary, paid dividend of **USD25,000** to its shareholders; took more Bank loan of **USD30,000** and bought the retiring shareholder's shares worth **USD50,000**

The cash generated from financing activity would thus be as follows:

	USD
Additional Bank loan	30,000
Dividend Received	5,000
Less: Dividend Payment	(25,000)
Share acquisition	(50,000)
Cash Generated from Financing Activity:	**(40,000)**

(v) The Net Cash Generated from business activity within 2019 for the SME should be:

	USD
Cash Generated from Operating Activity	**225,000**
Cash Generated from Investing Activity	**(150,000)**
Cash Generated from Financing Activity:	**(40,000)**
Net Cash Generated from Business Activity	**35,000**
Opening balance of cash and cash equivalent was	55,000

The Closing balance of cash and cash equivalent was USD90,000, which reconciled with **USD90,000 (USD35,000 + USD55,000).**

We have used the above simplified process to increase our understanding of the Cash Flow Analysis; because of its importance in effective handling of business. Virtually any item of cash movement one may ever encounter in any business, can be rightly categorized under one of the items highlighted in the above example of Cash Flow Analysis.

The Cash flow analyses is designed to enable businesses ensure their activities actually generate cash, *which constitutes the lifeline of every business.* It is not enough to declare profit, in addition to ensuring the business remains profitable. It is far more important for businesses to ensure the stated profits can be supported with sufficient cash generated from business. A liquid SME stand at vantage position; as it can easily meet its business financial demands at any time, can engage in investing activities as demonstrated by the SME in the above example.

A liquid SME can benefit from any golden opportunity that could come up along the line. *The liquid SME can easily meet its Transactionary needs, Precautionary motives, Speculative business needs, Future Requirement motives, and Compensating needs. These are according to the International Accounting Standards 3 provisions*

Some businesses, unfortunately went into sudden bankruptcy or liquidation; because there were no conscious efforts to pick the signals from the cash flow analysis and adjust the company accordingly. Every SME would require the necessary discipline to allow its process and operations to be subjected to standard Risk Management framework, which is vital for its sustainable growth.

Various companies and indeed SMEs have different rates profitability. It is corporate recklessness to be embarking on investment or financing activities that cannot be supported by the company's profitability nor liquidity. The resultant effect would be the compulsion to partly or heavily mortgage the firm to creditors. This of course, has been the most common cause of sudden collapse of some thriving entities. We strongly believe that your own business would not make that mistake, but should exploit the learning points from this book to maintain sustainable growth beyond your lifetime.

CHAPTER 12

SME Cash Cycle: *82% of start-ups fail because of poor cash flow.*

The Cash Cycle of a business is the average period it takes the company to commence a typical round of producing its products/services, till the point of receiving cash payments for the products and services. The following examples may assist to make it clearer:

(i) A manufacturer of Chocolates' cash cycle would be the average period it takes the company to source for its raw materials, produces the chocolates, takes the products through its storage facilities, sell the products to customers, either on credit or cash basis; till the point the full cash payments for the produced chocolates are received into the company. In some cases, it may take up to 30 days to source for raw materials and produce the products, and another 60 days to sell and receive cash payments for the goods. This would imply that the cash cycle for this entity is 90 days.

(ii) Another entity may be a Contractor that sources for its jobs through competitive bidding process that could last for weeks and an average period of 90 days to execute the project and another two to three months to receive full cash. The average cash cycle of this entity would thus be 180 days

(iii) Other entities involved in trading business may depend on importation of their goods. The average period of ordering and receiving the merchandise from abroad may be 30 days and another 30 days to sell the goods, while another 30 days is needed to receive the sales proceeds in cash. This means that the average cash cycle of this entity is 90 days.

Key to Sustainable SME by Chiedu Okonta

(v) There could be some other entities that purchase goods on cash basis from major importers and sell to end users and retailers on cash basis, but take about 30 days to complete the cash cycle.

(vi) There could be a food Vendor that sources for its raw materials and sells its entire goods with full cash receipt within 7 days. Hence the cash cycle here is 7 days.

Cash Turnover: This is the number of times a company's cash cycle is repeated in a year. For instance, an SME that has 180 days as its cash cycle, its cash turnover would be **2 times**. This is 360/180 days. In the same vein an SME that has 90 days as its cash cycle, its cash turnover would be **4 times**, which is 360/90. Also 120 days' cash cycle would imply **3 times** cash turnover; while 30 days' cash cycle gives cash turnover of **12 times;** and cash cycle of 6 days would imply cash turnover of **60 times.** Clearly, given the same line of business, the higher the cash turnover of a company, the more efficient that entity is over its rivals.

The shorter the cash cycle, the higher the cash turnover, and all things being equal, the higher the profitability and liquidity. The cash cycle of every company would depend on the level of financial management services required to increase its efficiency, which include various strategies to reduce the cash cycle. This is because, the longer the cash cycle, the more the need to consider various funding opportunities to reduce the cash cycle.

The following are some of the ways to reduce cash cycle:

(1). SALES DISCOUNTS: Sales discounts have been a major means of encouraging customers to patronize the company and pay promptly for their goods/services. From the above examples we saw some customers take between 30 days and 90 days to pay for goods/services sold to them. The tool of cash discounts is designed to reduce this 30 to 90 days waiting period.

In Accounting the sales discounts may be stated as:

(i). **5% 10 Net 30.** This means that the customers are encouraged to pay within 10 days and obtain **5%** cash discount, else, the sales proceeds should be paid for within 30 days in full. From **Chapter 6,** we understand that credit sales must satisfy some basic due diligence standards. If the customer fails to pay within 10 days, the SME loses the discount. This means that for the 20 days **(30-10)** in that month, the SME loses **5%** benefit of discount, which would translate to total of **90% (5% *360/20)** loss of cash discount per annum. Since the SME can easily obtain loan at less than **90%** interest per annum, it would be better for the SME to always pay within 10 days using banking loan to bridge the funding gap.

(ii). **4% 10 Net 30:** From the above explanation, the **4%** cash sales discount implies the SME must pay for the goods within 10 days. Failure of which would imply annual loss of **72% (4% *360/20)** cash discount annually. If the SME is sure to obtain banking loan at less than **72%** annual interest, then it is advisable to utilize the cash discount by using banking loan to bridge the funding gap.

(iii). **3% 10 Net 30:** In the same vein, If the SME fails to pay within 10 days, it forfeits the 3% discount, which results in **54% (3% * 360/20) loss of cash discounts per annum.** As long as the SME can access facility at less than 54% per annum, it's advisable to accept the discount while the gap should be settled by business loan.

(iv). **2% 10 Net 30:** Loss of discount here, would imply annual loss of **36% (2% * 360/20).** Same advice as in **(i) to (iii)** above

NOTE:

The above advice is on the assumption that the products/services involved have ready market and that the SME's customers buy and pay up within 30 days.

(2). CREDIT PURCHASES

In addition to using cash discounts to manage cash cycle, the SME may find credit purchases very useful. This is a situation where the SME suppliers allow the SME to buy the goods and pay later at a future date. This is an interest free loan and it is highly recommended for the SME. This is provided that the goods are in the normal course of the SME's business, for which the SME has the required demand for the goods, as well as the capacity to ensure the goods are promptly sold and cash recovered.

Making Account Payable longer: Financial Analysts have in time past postulated that SMEs are encouraged to extend the time of paying for their Accounts Payable. For example, that if the SME has the policy to pay its Accounts Payable 30 or 60 or 90 days after work, then, the fund would boost working capital during that period.

Further attempts were made to calculate the gains the SME would make per annum for implementing such policies. In today's competitive and digital age, such policies have proven to be counter- productive in the long run, and as such no longer recommended for SMEs. This is essentially because both the SME and its Suppliers, Vendors, Contractors and in fact customers are all in the open market; and can always access suitable alternatives.

(3). Early Payments of Bills

In order to allow your SME, build competitive advantage over others in todays' world, it must strive to pay its bills early! This practice would leave positive and long-lasting impression for your SME in the minds of its Vendors. This would facilitate the retention of the SME as the preferred entity, including receipts of various forms of discounts. Enormous amounts of resources can be conserved for the SME by receiving good discounts from all your Vendors. **Please see the topic on sales discounts above.** The company should strive to pay all Vendors on time. If for any reason, the SME is unable to meet the deadline, then it must inform the Vendors on time. The Vendors are more likely to understand and accept such occasional lapses, especially if it is not the pattern.

(4). Maintain Good Relationship with Vendors

It is so vital for the SME to keep and maintain good relationship with all its Vendors. This would delight the Vendors and enhance the SME retention, including having opportunities to receive better and mouth-watering offers, and enticing discounts. In case of unexpected business exigencies, this mutual relationship would assist the SMEs to obtain quick responses from their Vendors. These benefits would reduce the actual costs of the SMEs businesses and ultimately increase value for the SMEs.

(5). There Must Be Strong Internal Control Process Against Fraud

Through internal collaboration, manipulation of Accounts Payable and Accounts Receivable are the major channels of fraud in an organisation. This category of fraud usually gets entrenched in the system and it is so difficult to detect and/or eliminate due to its high secrecy and subtlety.

There could be mark ups in Vendor fees, inflation of Vendor prices, and payments to Vendors for work not done.

The best way to prevent this dishonest process is to ensure inbuilt strong internal control procedures that promotes:

- ✓ Separation of duties;
- ✓ Use of pre-set limits of graduated approval authorities;
- ✓ Increased number of approval authorities; and
- ✓ Established due diligence procedure for introducing, engaging, monitoring, evaluating, and paying Vendors, in the organisation.

So many SMEs struggling with high cost of operations today and low/no profitability may actually be suffering due to over invoicing from manipulation of Accounts Payable. The strong Internal Control Process should include, but not limited to the following factors:

- There must be a Database of Vendors enlisted in the organisation;

- The enlistment of the Vendors must be subjected to pre selection and pre- qualification conditions;

- The pre-selection must be opened to competitive bidding that involve multiple Vendors being selected under clearly defined pre- qualification criteria;

- Pre-qualification of Vendors must disclose the ultimate beneficial owner of the Vendor company, with evidence of verifiable means of identification. It should also disclose relevant experience in the field of duty;

- The approval authorities should be graduated according to the level of Vendors services and value involved;

- The Internal Control process must allow segregation of duties such that; at least two or three Officers must be involved and agree before a transaction takes place;

- There should be independent review of Accounts Payable transactions by Quality Assurance Officers to revalidate the invoices with actual goods/services obtained versus the amounts paid to Vendors;

- There must be consequent management against any Officer who flouts the established internal control process in handling Vendors account;

- The consequent management for any Officer that will defraud the company; directly by violating the internal policies, or indirectly by collaborating or colluding with Vendor/Customer/Supplier/Outsider to cheat the organisation; in any form, shall be by terminal sanction, excluding judicial prosecution.

6. On no Account Should Vendors Invoices be paid Before Receiving Products or Services!

The Internal Control Process must be such that an independent Officer should validate the product or service supplied, to confirm that the Vendor and the products/services supplied, conformed with the set due diligence in the organisation, prior to releasing funds to Vendors. The check should confirm that the Vendor was duly authorised, the quality, quantity and amount of goods/services supplied are consistent with what was pre-approved.

7. Automation of Account Payable Process

Imagine what happens if an organisation automates its medical care cost, such that every medical expense can be traced to actual medical care authorised by medical practitioner, charged against a staff within its predetermined limit? Or every stationery utilised is traced to staff usage rather than stock piling of stationery? The more paperless an organisation becomes, the easier it is to effectively manage its Accounts Payable. This would enable all the process, including the approval and payment functions, to become automated, hence it eliminates the usual human sentiments associated with approving and paying of Vendors bills.

Automation of the Accounts Payable process, especially where it involves routine need to order bulk purchases from suppliers, the Vendors can simply be linked into your Accounts Payable and inventory network; by means of a Supplier/Vendor portal. This process would promote seamless monitoring and tracking of inventory supplies and automate Vendors payments.

Efficient Inventory Production Management

It does not matter what line of business your entity is involved in; whether it is production of goods, or offering of services; efficient inventory production management is the process of improving the cash cycle. The process enables the SME to review its line of business to reduce the time it takes to ordinarily collect cash from its customers. A Church for instance, may adopt the use of technology, such that members may not need to wait till Sunday service or month end to pay their tithes. With an automated App, members can make such payments directly online.

Other service industry can have the automated App that enables their clients to make direct payments upon signing the contract, while the other instalments are transferred automatically, once the agreed threshold is achieved.

In the same way, for an organization involved in production of goods, an automated App can be set up that allows the customers, Suppliers and the SME to be linked together; such that all can monitor the production and inventory, which enables the customers make direct transfers ahead of, and during production, and receive goods once produced.

Effective Management of Account Receivables

Effective management of Accounts Receivables is similar to all the factors enumerated above on effective management of Accounts Payable. Typically, Accounts Receivables are the SME customers that buy goods/services on credit and are given predetermined terms of settlement. Depending on the SME and the agreement terms, some customers may have up to 90 days, or 60 days, or 30 days or less to settle their purchases. As indicated earlier, **the SME cash cycle is the average time it takes the SME to completely produce its goods/services, sell them and collect its money from customers.** The longer the time is, the less efficient the SME is in managing its cash cycle. This is because, the longer the cash cycle, the more the need to consider various funding opportunities to reduce the cash cycle.

Below are some of the ways to use effective management of Account Receivable in reducing cash cycle period:

(1). SALES DISCOUNTS: Sales discounts has been a major means of encouraging customers to patronize the company and pay promptly for their goods/services. From the above examples we saw some customers take between 30 days and 90 days to pay for goods/services sold to them. The tool of cash discounts is designed to reduce this 30 to 90 days waiting period.

Key to Sustainable SME by Chiedu Okonta

In Accounting the sales discounts may be stated as:

(i). **5% 10 Net 30.** This means that the customers are encouraged to pay within 10 days and obtain **5%** cash discount, else, the sales proceeds should be paid within 30 days in full. From **Chapter 6,** we understand that credit sales must satisfy some basic due diligence standards. If the customer fails to pay within 10 days, the customer loses the discount. This means that for the 20 days **(30-10)** in that month, the customer loses **5%** benefit of discount, which would translate to total of **90% (5% *360/20)** loss of cash discount per annum.

Since the customer can easily obtain loan at less than **90%** interest per annum, it would be better for the SME to encourage the customer to pay within 10 days; using banking loan to bridge the funding gap. The SME may get all its major customers to patronize the same bank with the SME, so that the Bank can easily grant the SME customers short term loans to bridge the funding gap. This practice would greatly improve the cash cycle of the SME.

(ii). **4% 10 Net 30:** From the above explanation, the **4%** cash sales discount implies the that SMEs customers must pay for the goods within 10 days. Failure of which would imply annual loss of **72% (4% *360/20)** cash discount. As explained in (i) above, the SME should encourage its customers to pay within 10 days using banking loan to bridge the funding gap.

(iii). **3% 10 Net 30:** In the same vein, If the SME customer fails to pay within 10 days, it forfeits the 3% discount, which results in **54% (3% * 360/20)** per annum interest. The SME should encourage its customers to pay within 10 days using banking loan to bridge the funding gap, having gained **54%** interest per annum.

(iv). **2% 10 Net 30:** Loss of discount here, would imply annual loss of **36% (2% * 360/20).** Same advice as in **(i) to (iii)** above

CREDIT SALES WITHOUT DISCOUNTS & OTHER CONDITIONS

In spite of the practice of granting discounts, there may still be some SME customers that would fail to utilize the discounts. Using Accounts Receivables to improve the cash cycle, the following processes are recommended:

(i). For any customer to qualify as a credit customer, the following minimum standard must have been fulfilled. Proper profiling, character assessment, complete documentation of the customer's details and compliance with the SME's due diligence.

(ii) There should be a Database of all customers of the SME with unique identification for each credit customer;

(iii). There must be proper prior authorization for every credit sale;

(iv). For every credit customer that fails to pay up after 14 days, there should be a formal communication to the customer reminding the customer to pay up:

(vii) At the end of 30 days another formal letter should be written to the customer to pay up, which should be followed up with reminders after every two weeks

(viii) It is important to ensure that for every credit sale, the due diligence requirement should have taken suitable collateral, such that failure to meet the obligation on due dates, the collateral should automatically become forfeited for the SME.

CHAPTER 13

Best Investments Handling Procedure

No individual, nor business entity, nor a people, nor a nation, can attain sustainable growth without deliberate and conscious efforts to grow investments!

A staunch believer in the value-based investing model, investment guru **Warren Buffett** started investing at the age of 11, and said he wished he had started earlier. We understand that even *"**God teaches us to make profit**"* (Isaiah 48:17); but in Joshua 1:8 and Isaiah 48:15 God declares that *"**you shall make your way prosperous**"* So making one's way prosperous is each individual's personal responsibility and it is mandatory.

Failure to imbibe the habit of savings/investments is mostly driven by the assumption that it is optional. From the above examples, and from Proverbs 4:18 *"**... the path of the just is like a shining light that shines more and more unto the perfect day**"* it becomes clear that savings/investments is mandatory for every individual, business entity, a people, and a nation; if the dream of sustainable growth is to be achieved!

This can be easily understood by looking at African nations, from time to time, some African nations witnessed purposeful leadership that focussed on investment/developments, and almost automatically, economic growth is witnessed in such nations. But when the leadership of such nation shifts focus from investments/developments, retardation, retrogressions and poverty ensue.

Without savings, investments may be hindered and without investments there cannot be sustainable growth. Savings is the practice of setting aside part of current earnings for future uses, while investment is the process of putting resources in income-yielding venture. In other words, investments is making your money work for you, such that in addition to your principal amount invested, you earn a premium called profit or interest!

The best form of savings is the savings that is combined with investments. This is why insurance savings as a typical form of savings, is less preferred to savings in money market investments that has the capacity to grow at compounded interest rate.

Investment decisions may involve three major types as follows:

1. Long term investment decisions from regular low stream of income

Using a hypothetical assumption that, **Joyce** graduated from her Master's Degree at age 22 years and commenced savings from her first pay with monthly contributions 5% of her salary, while the employer contributes 7.5% of her salary into a Mutual Funds at 4% per annum, compounded monthly. She was so disciplined that additional salary increase of USD2,000/month after three years of engagement, and subsequently after every three years, until she became 30 years; was fully invested in the Mutual Fund. Given that the investment was growing at 4% interest per annum and there was no other increase in monthly contribution till retirement age, JOYCE should have made the following investment growth:

Age	Monthly Salary USD	5% Cont	7.5% Cont	Total Cont	4% FV @ Rtmt USD
22	2,000	100	150	250	13,390.16
45	6,000	4,300	450	4,750	1,528,187
50	6,000	4,300	450	4,750,	2,167,571
60	6,000	4,300	450	4,750	3,901,473
70	6,000	4,300	450	4,750	6,806,309

I am sure as you are seeing this, if you are an employee that has failed to utilize this golden opportunity, or you believed as an entrepreneur, you could have easily made similar investments, which you did not do; you would be feeling so pained as I did. Especially as you can easily see that Joyce still had other part of her salary to spend, just the discipline to invest and to know where to invest. The power of monthly compounding of return is what Warren Buffet refers to as *'the 8th Myth of the world'.*

The good news is that **Today is not too late to commence your value adding investment.** Though I started late, but very soon, I shall also be counted among the league of great investors. You do not need to make the mistake others made: Warren Buffet started at age 11 and wished he had started earlier. It means any person up to 11 years should have started. Parents with under age children below 11 years are in the best position to commence savings/investments plan for each of their children, such that the normal pressure and harassments for sponsoring children through University education would not be a challenge to you.

CAUTION! CAUTION!! CAUTION!!!

The acid test of every good investment is that it must meet the following qualifications:

(i) **It must be backed by underlying business fundamentals:** Any investment that should attract your attention must have the basic business fundamentals. It is not every investment that results in good returns. Some investments may even promise great returns, but in actual fact, do not. If it were only based on promises, **Ponzi schemes would have been the best investments, but they are not, and neither can they.** The business fundamental should include well known product/service being sold to a ready market with good margin. The minimum requirement should be that the company being invested in should have been making sufficient profit to pay dividend and have extra income left for the business growth. Or it can be substantially shown that the business can achieve good profits and dividend payments.

(ii) **The entry and exit from the investment should be seamless:** The investor should be able to exit at will or upon maturity. There are some environments that would promise attractive returns on investment, but their foreign regulations would not allow the investor to exit at will. If care is not taken, it may be difficult to recover the investments upon maturity.

(iii) **Management:** Any company that should be invested in must have an established structure with strong corporate governance in place. The top management must consist of staff with requisite skills and experience, whose past pedigrees are impeccable and worthy of the trust. It should be a company that has the practice of paying dividend and reinvesting its reserve funds into the business pursuits. The management structure and the track record of such company should be transparent enough, to disclose where they have failed, while still reporting their gains.

(iv) **Financial measures:** Any company that is worthy of your investment must have the compelling financial performance over a period that places the company among the top entities in terms of return on investments. An entity that has a pattern of generating sufficient Profit to be reinvested into the reserve fund for business expansion after paying taxes and dividend, is most preferable as your investment choice.

(v) **Value:** Here attention is paid to the intrinsic value of the company you are investing in. The company must have such unique value, which stands out as its competitive advantage over similar companies in the industry. The advantage of this quality is that it points to the entity's continued success in business. It speaks to the extent customers would continue to patronise the goods/services of the company because of its uniqueness.

2. Investment in short and long term assets

Investment may be made in shares, or in mutual fund, Treasury bills, or any other money market products, or in real estate, for the purpose of taking profit within a short or long term. Investments should naturally be for a long term, but opportunities that emerged within a short term may be utilized. The major attractions from this set of investments are investment appreciation and interest benefits. In order to maximize gains from this set of investments the following factors should be considered:

(i). Due diligence review: The required due diligence process highlighted in this book should be considered before embarking on these investments.

(ii). Risk Appetite: The investor should define its tolerable limits of risk. It is the level below which you are unwilling to lose money from your investments. It is normal for value of investments to rise and fall from time to time, depending on the market forces and the viability of the investments. The investor is expected to make his gains from the movement in prices of these investments, they are not supposed to be the cause for worry. However, each investor should review his investment and know the maximum loss he is capable of accepting from a particular investment and be prepared to respond accordingly.

(iii). Diversification: A very good investment principle is to ensure a well-diversified investment portfolio. This is a process of spreading the investment risk among the pool of available investment channels. For an investor that has an XUSD amount for investment, it's advisable to have spread his investment in shares, mutual funds, Treasury bills and real estate. Even in the same line of investment; like shares, diversification is highly recommended. If all the investments in shares are only in one organization, any unfortunate occurrence against that company would affect the investor. The same applies to all other forms of investment, hence the need to spread the risk.

(iv). Knowledge of the Investments: In the words of Mr Tony Elumelu (CON) *"You cannot market what you do not know"* There are so many things calling for the attention of everyone that has the resources to invest in. An investor is not expected to delve into an area of investment, for which he/she does not have the basic knowledge of the market. It is a big risk to do so. During the stock market boom of 2007, many people, including smaller business owners, working class etc. sold their other businesses and assets to invest in shares, without the basic knowledge of the stock market. In order to ensure sustainable growth in any business, every investor should focus on the areas he/she has sufficient knowledge about. The investor should have at least, a fair knowledge of the market he has invested in. Be it money market, or stock market or real estate market

(v). Have Control of the Investments: In addition to being knowledgeable about what you are investing in; the investor should have reasonable control over his investment. For example, an investor should have access to his investment statement of account regularly, and he should actively participate in the decision to withdraw or increase the investment. Whether the investment is in capital market, or money market, or real estate market, the investor should be part of his investment decisions at all times.

(vi). Must be Involved in the Investment Decisions: The investor's knowledge and control over his business, would still require his involvement in managing his investment. If it is shares for instance, he must take interest in the stock market, and be involved in what shares, and when to buy or sell decisions. The investor in real estate should be involved in knowing the environment, as well as the structure of his investment

ENVIRONMENTAL IMPACT TO SUSTAINABLE SMEs

Notwithstanding everything written in this book, the environment has a significant impact on the extent the SMEs can achieve sustainable growth. There are some basic socio –economic infrastructures that are necessary for the SMEs to thrive, the absence of which constitutes major challenge against the success of the SMEs. The following are examples of such infrastructures:

- Uninterrupted electricity supply
- Good network of roads
- Secured environment, where the rule of law is supreme
- Constant supply of portable water
- Quality education to all citizens to at least up to secondary school level
- Less import dependent
- Reduced burden of foreign debt

"Any government that cannot guarantee its citizens, at least the availability of the above top 5 socio- economic infrastructures, which are minimum requirement for citizens' existence is not qualified to be" (Lee Kuan Yew- Prime Minister of Singapore 1959 - 1990).

The absence of the above infrastructure in most developing nations, especially in Africa has resulted in several challenges among which are:

- High cost of production

- Low life expectancy

- High unemployment

- Low pa capital income

- High rate of poverty

- High Import dependency in the midst of absence or low local production

- High burden of foreign debt without the expected accompanying productive sector

- High rate of political violence as the illiterates become ready tools for electioneering violence.

Considering the enormous benefits that nations would have achieved both in the short and long run for allowing the basic socio-economic infrastructures to be in place, as well as the hardships associated with not having those infrastructures, one really wonders why any government would make such mistakes? The actual cost of meeting the infrastructural goal/objective is far less than the cost the nations have to bear for failing to meet them. ''**According to the World Bank report, Nigeria loses $28 Billion annually to power shortages**''.

If you take this for the past **30 years, that is $840 Billion.** When you aggregate it by adding the lack of constant water supply and good network of roads; it would be by far more than the foreign loans the country has been struggling to take and service!

The good news is: that as manifested by several great African entrepreneurs, Christian leaders, and few Political leaders; ***everything required for the sustainable growth of Africa is in Africa!*** Many manufacturing outfits can successfully operate in Africa with 100% local raw materials and indigenous contents.

Every individual, family, SME and indeed nation in Africa, should rise up urgently to embrace sustainable SME growth, and thus boost our respective nations' economic growth and development.

CONTACT

RIVERGATE ONYX INVESTMENTS LTD: Experts in Financial Management & Consulting Services.

Website : www.chiedurivergate.com
Telephone : +233540110060; 0592303276
Email : chieduknt@yahoo.com
Designer: Prince Ayettey: +233262928083

REFERENCES

1. World Bank Report of 2018 & 2019
2. Africapitalism Philosophy- Tony O Elumelu (CON)
3. SME Competitiveness in Ghana Alliances for Action 2016
4. Nigerian Bureau of Statistics Report on African Businesses
5. ME Financial Health
6. Office for Advocacy
7. OECD Library
8. Bureau of Labour Statistics (Feb 28th 2020)
9. Valuer + by Katrina Aaslaid
10. Finance Basic for Managers Harvard Business Review
11. Chartered Institute of Management Accounting CIMA- Fraud Risk Management Guide
12. Managing Up and Across –Harvard Business Review
13. Building Your Business – Harvard Business Review
14. World Bank SME Finance
15. International Accounting Standards IAS
16. Small Business Administration (SBA)-Office of Advocacy 2018
17. Warren Buffett's Investing Strategy